Making Friends for Jesus

(For the full story, read Acts 9 verses 1-28)

Dear Friend

HUNT&
THORPE

Written and illustrated by Peter Rogers

WARNING!

Damascus was on full "red-alert"! There couldn't be anyone who wasn't aware that Paul was on his way.

Paul was a bully. Wherever he went there was trouble and that was bad news for the people of Damascus and especially bad news for Jesus' friends.

But what the people of Damascus didn't know was that Jesus was planning to meet Paul on the way. That was good news for Paul and very good news for Jesus' friends!

Z

That night, in Damascus, one of Jesus' friends lay sleeping, tucked up warm and cosy in his bed. As he slept, Jesus spoke to him in a dream:

"Ananias!"

"Yes, Lord?"

"Tomorrow, I want you to go and pray for a new friend of mine called Paul."

"Did you say Paul, Lord?"

"Yes, that's right, Paul, do you know him?"

"Er, yes, Lord. Sort of. Isn't he the one that has sworn to put anyone who claims to be one of your friends in prison, or even worse, to death!"

"Yes, that's the one."

"Are you sure, Lord? Don't you think it might be just a little dangerous to go and pray for this man?"

"ANANIAS!"

"Yes, Lord!"

"Thank you."

Tap Tap

And so it was that an obedient but rather worried Ananias knocked on the door of the house where Paul was staying. Surprised and quite relieved to be greeted by an unusually quiet and rather humble Paul, his heart warmed as he remembered what Jesus had asked him to do, and he smiled. Ananias gave Paul a great big hug and began to pray for him.

Paul felt like a new man. Now that he knew who Jesus was and what he could do, Paul wanted everyone else to get to know him.

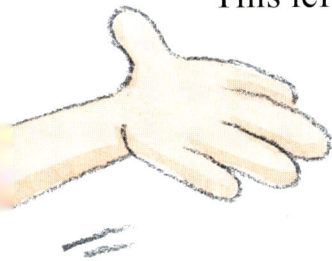

This left the poor townspeople feeling very confused, especially Jesus' friends. It certainly wasn't what they were expecting to hear from him.

Mind you, this wasn't the Paul they were expecting to see either. He certainly appeared to have changed!

And this 'new Paul' got some very different reactions...

"People like that don't just change over night." Said some.

"He's just pretending, so that he can make friends with us and then have us beaten up and thrown into prison." Said others.

But others took their feelings a bit further. A small group of men, who were totally against Jesus and furious with Paul for changing sides, decided to give him a taste of his own medicine and remove him for good!

Paul's friends wanted him to stay,
but feared for his life. So, sadly, they encouraged
him to leave. But how? Paul's enemies were
waiting at every gate that led out of the city.
There was no means of escape - or was there?

The answer was simple, but risky! (Especially for someone who didn't like heights.) If he couldn't pass through the city wall by one of the many gates then he would have to go over it!

That night, Paul made his escape. With the help of some friends, he nervously climbed into a large basket which they then very slowly and very carefully lowered down the outside of the wall.

Paul was *very* relieved to land safely, *very* happy to be out of the city and *very* grateful to his friends for their help. The landing certainly wouldn't have been so gentle without them!

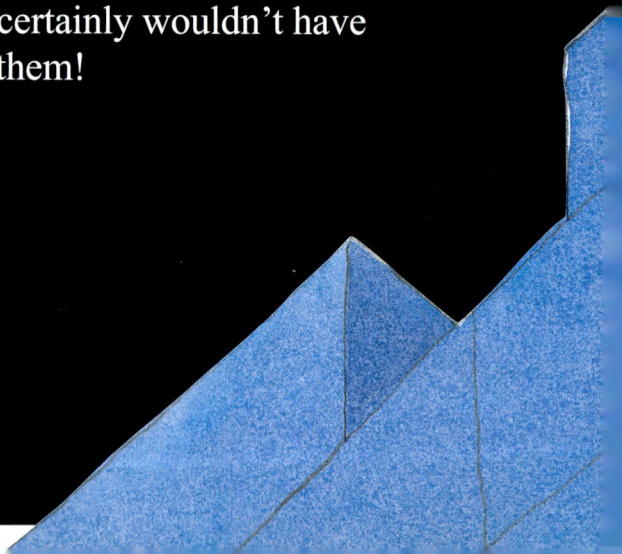

"Mummy!"

"Gulp!"

Paul made his way back to Jerusalem just as fast as he could, only to be greeted with the same fear and suspicion he had experienced in Damascus.

It was simply too much for anyone to believe that Paul could possibly have become a friend of Jesus.

All, that is, except for one...

"Barnabas! What have you done?" Exclaimed Peter, James and a number of other special friends of Jesus who were hiding in Jerusalem.

"You must be off your head, he's dangerous!"

"This is our new friend Paul" said Barnabas, "he's changed."

"But how can you be so sure?" They all said.

"Because I've talked with him and I've heard how he met with Jesus. I've also seen the difference in the way he lives".

After Barnabas had told them the whole story, they were delighted to realise is was all true. They made Paul very welcome and encouraged him to tell his story all over Jerusalem. It all led to some very exciting adventures. But that's another story.